NATIONAL GEOGRAPHIC

READINGS ABOUT AMERIC

The SOUTHEAST Today

PICTURE CREDITS
Cover Carl & Ann Purcell/Corbis; pages 1, 5 (middle), 25 JH Pete Carmichael; pages 2–3 Roger Ressmeyer/Corbis; pages 4–5 Kevin Fleming/Corbis; page 5 (top) Jack Gurner; pages 6–7 William A. Bake/Corbis; page 7 Buddy Mays/Corbis; page 8 John Springer Collection/Corbis; pages 8–9, 12, 29 Raymond Gehman/Corbis; page 9 Charles Lajeunesse/Photo-Bytes (DBA)/Lajeunesse Business Associates; pages 10–11, 11 (right) Galen Rowell/Corbis; page 11 (left) Royalty-Free/Corbis; pages 12–13 Patrick Ward/Corbis; page 13 Earl & Nazima Kowall/Corbis; page 15 (top) Bob Gathany/U.S. Space Camp Huntsville, AL; page 15 (bottom) Joseph Sohm; ChromoSohm Inc./Corbis; pages 16, 17 Richard T. Nowitz/Corbis; page 18 Richard Cummins/Corbis; pages 19, 20 (bottom left), 21 Philip Gould/Corbis; page 22 (bottom) Nathan Benn/Corbis; page 23 Michele Westmoreland/AGE Fotostock; page 24 Royalty-Free/Corbis; pages 24–25 Taxi/Getty Images; page 30 Courtesy of Habitat for Humanity; page 31 (top) Mark Peterson/Corbis; page 31 (bottom) Robert Maass/Corbis; page 32 (top, middle) Bob Krist/Corbis; page 32 (bottom) Alain Le Garsmeur/Corbis.

cover: Seagulls in St. Petersburg, Florida

pages 2–3: Space shuttle launch from Cape Canaveral, Florida

Produced through the worldwide resources of the National Geographic Society, John M. Fahey, Jr., President and Chief Executive Officer; Gilbert M. Grosvenor, Chairman of the Board; Nina D. Hoffman, Executive Vice President and President, Books and Education Publishing Group.

PREPARED BY NATIONAL GEOGRAPHIC SCHOOL PUBLISHING
Ericka Markman, Senior Vice President and President, Children's Books and Education Publishing Group; Steve Mico, Senior Vice President and Publisher; Marianne Hiland, Executive Editor; Anita Schwartz, Project Editor; Jim Hiscott, Design Manager; Kristin Hanneman, Illustrations Manager; Diana Bourdrez, Picture Editor; Matt Wascavage, Manager of Publishing Services; Sean Philpotts, Production Manager.

MANUFACTURING AND QUALITY MANAGEMENT
Christopher A. Liedel, Chief Financial Officer; Phillip L. Schlosser, Director; Clifton M. Brown III, Manager.

PROGRAM DEVELOPMENT Gare Thompson Associates, Inc.

ART DIRECTION Dan Banks, Project Design Company

CONSULTANTS/REVIEWERS
Dr. Margit E. McGuire, School of Education, Seattle University, Seattle, Washington

BOOK DEVELOPMENT Nieman Inc.

BOOK DESIGN Three Communication Design, LLC

MAP DEVELOPMENT AND PRODUCTION Dave Stevenson

Published by the National Geographic Society
1145 17th Street, N.W.
Washington, D.C. 20036-4688

ISBN: 0-7922-4533-4

Fourth Printing September 2009
Printed in Canada

CoNTENTs

The SOUTHEAST

The Southeast is the place for you if you like warmth. It has sunny weather, friendly people, spicy food, and lively music. The Southeast is varied, a home to both old traditions and new technology. To learn the answers to the following questions—and a lot of other interesting things about the Southeast—read on.

Where on **Earth** can you feel like you're on the **moon**?

Find out on page 15.

What is **zydeco** music?

Find out on page 21.

ARKANSAS

MISSISSIPPI

LOUISIANA

N
W   E
S

How did **Casey Jones** become a **railroad legend**?
Find out on page 26.

What's a **flamingo tongue** when it's not part of a bird?
Find out on page 25.

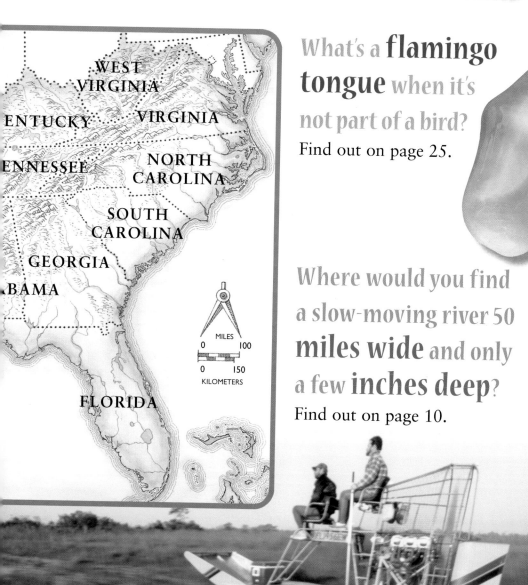

WEST VIRGINIA

KENTUCKY

VIRGINIA

TENNESSEE

NORTH CAROLINA

SOUTH CAROLINA

GEORGIA

ALABAMA

FLORIDA

MILES
0   100

0   150
KILOMETERS

Where would you find a slow-moving river 50 **miles wide** and only a few **inches deep**?
Find out on page 10.

Touring the Southeast

By Lisa Moran

You can find many great places to visit in the Southeast. Here are two spots that are full of surprises. One is an area of beautiful mountains with natural springs where the water is really hot! The other spot is a big city that was the birthplace of rock and roll.

Fog covering the Ozark Mountains

The Ozarks

One of the great wilderness areas of the Southeast is the Ozark National Forest. It's located in northwestern Arkansas in the Ozark Mountains. You can stay in a log cabin in the woods and hike one of the many trails. The Ozarks also have many beautiful streams and lakes. In fact, one of the most popular water activities here is *floating*—in canoes, kayaks, rafts, or johnboats. Johnboats are flat-bottomed boats used for fishing. There are lots of fish, such as trout and bass, if you want to try your luck.

Arkansas has many natural hot springs—places where hot, clear spring water rises up out of the ground. The town of Hot Springs has 47 springs, spouting 800,000 gallons of water every day. The water temperature can get as high as 147 degrees Fahrenheit. That's hotter than your bath or shower.

Be sure to take a trip up Hot Springs Mountain to Hot Springs Tower. You can ride an elevator to the top of the tower for a view of the surrounding lakes, mountains, and valleys. On a clear day, you can see for 40 miles.

Memphis

About 180 miles northeast of Hot Springs is Memphis, the largest city in Tennessee. Memphis sits on the banks of the Mississippi River. The city is most famous for its music. It was the home of the "King of Rock and Roll," Elvis Presley. Elvis recorded his first two records in Memphis at Sun Studio, which is still there.

Elvis's famous mansion, Graceland, is just outside of downtown Memphis. You can see his lavish rooms, sparkling costumes, and gold records. Be sure to stop at Meditation Gardens, where Elvis is buried.

Another Memphis stop is Mud Island. You can take a monorail or walkway to this 52-acre island park. On the island, the Mississippi River Museum shows life on the river. Outside the museum is the River Walk, a model of the Mississippi River that is five blocks long.

◀ Elvis Presley performing in 1957

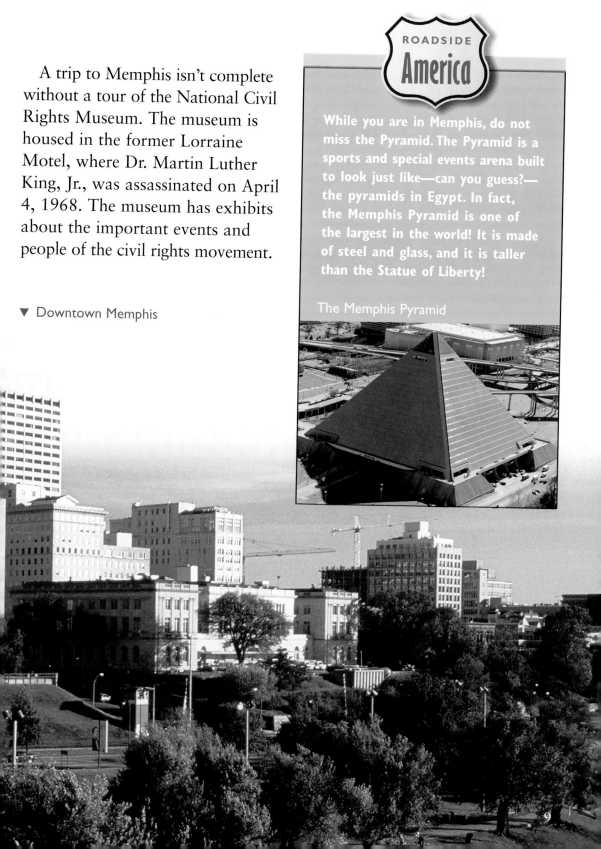

A trip to Memphis isn't complete without a tour of the National Civil Rights Museum. The museum is housed in the former Lorraine Motel, where Dr. Martin Luther King, Jr., was assassinated on April 4, 1968. The museum has exhibits about the important events and people of the civil rights movement.

▼ Downtown Memphis

While you are in Memphis, do not miss the Pyramid. The Pyramid is a sports and special events arena built to look just like—can you guess?—the pyramids in Egypt. In fact, the Memphis Pyramid is one of the largest in the world! It is made of steel and glass, and it is taller than the Statue of Liberty!

The Memphis Pyramid

The River of GRASS

By Liz West

The huge Florida wetland known as the Everglades is a slow-moving river 50 miles wide but only a few inches deep. People call the Everglades a "river of grass" because sawgrass covers most of it. Sawgrass is not really grass. It is a plant that has leaves edged with tiny sharp teeth that can easily cut through clothes—and skin!

Travel in the Everglades is difficult. You cannot wade through because the sawgrass will cut you. The water is too shallow for regular boats. So, we use an airboat. An airboat is a flat, open boat. Like an airplane, it has a big propeller to move it. The propeller is mounted on the rear of the boat. It makes a tremendous racket, but it does the job. The boat skims along the water's surface. Although we can still get lost in an airboat, at least we are above the alligators.

While hundreds of different kinds of animals live in the Everglades, the most famous is surely the alligator. Once endangered, 'gators are now protected within Everglades National Park. Visitors are likely to see them both on land and in water.

A full-grown alligator has few natural enemies. Adults can reach 19 feet. But do not let their large size fool you. They can still move very quickly on land. An alligator can reach speeds of 30 miles per hour.

Alligators are **reptiles,** or cold-blooded animals. Their body temperature changes with the outside temperature. To save energy, they **hibernate,** or sleep, during cold weather. They stop eating, and they often dig burrows. They stay there to keep warm during cold weather.

Everglades hunters: (left) a tricolored heron amid sawgrass and (above) an alligator

Protecting the Everglades

For a long time, dangers have threatened the Everglades. Around 1900, some people felt this precious wetland should be drained. They said it was just a big swamp and not good for anything. In the 1920s, there was a land boom in Florida. People wanted to build homes everywhere, including in the Everglades. They built canals, **levees**, and other water systems that stopped the rivers flowing into the Everglades.

Factories were built near rivers that flowed into the wetland. These factories dumped **toxic** waste that damaged the Everglades **ecosystem**.

People are now working to preserve the Everglades National Park for the future. One effort is the South Florida Research Center. The Center studies different problems that affect the Everglades area. Right now, one big problem is the paperbark tree. This tree is an invader from Australia.

New buildings affect the Everglades ecosystem.

Paperbark trees soak up a lot of water. In the early 1900s, people brought them to Florida because they thought they would help drain the Everglades. However, the invaders adapted too well. Paperbark trees have taken over hundreds of thousands of acres of the Everglades and killed other trees. Scientists are cutting down these invaders or spraying them with **herbicides** to kill them.

Other scientists are studying the canals and levees. They want to see how they can redirect them so that water flows more freely into the Everglades.

Words for You

ecosystem all the plants and animals that make up a natural community

herbicide a chemical that kills plants

hibernate to sleep during cold weather

levee a raised embankment built along a river to keep it from overflowing

reptile a cold-blooded animal

toxic poisonous

Blast Off!

By Aaron Zimmerman

When kids go away to camp, they usually play sports, go swimming and canoeing, take hikes, and do crafts. Space Camp at the U.S. Space and Rocket Center in Huntsville, Alabama, is different. There, kids learn all about space exploration. They also get a chance to do some of the things that **astronauts** do. For example, they use training **simulators** that help prepare astronauts for space flight.

Since 1982, more than 400,000 kids have taken part. Arriving for their five-day adventure, Space Campers are divided into groups of 15. Each team member is then given a job to do, similar to the ones that real astronauts have. The commander, for example, is in charge of launching the shuttle and **orbiting** Earth from space. (Real shuttles travel about 17,600 miles per hour!)

Other campers are assigned to work in Mission Control. They help the space shuttle communicate with Earth from about 150 nautical miles away.

One of the coolest experiences at Space Camp is finding out what it feels like to be in outer space. The moon is much smaller than Earth, and has far less **gravity**.

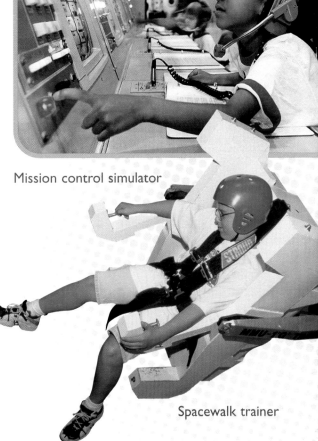

Mission control simulator

Spacewalk trainer

That is the force that pulls objects toward one another. So, people visiting the moon weigh about one-sixth of their Earth weight when they get there.

What does that feel like? To find out, campers are strapped into something called the 1/6th Gravity Chair. Soon, they're bouncing high and taking giant steps across a rocky surface similar to that of the moon.

15

Campers learn how to operate the controls of a spaceship.

Living in Space

Kids at Space Camp also learn what it is like to live on the International Space Station. The astronauts who really live there stay in space for many months at a time. Before going to sleep, they have to strap themselves to a bunk bed or to the wall. When they brush their teeth, they cannot spit, or their saliva would go flying around the space station. Instead, they have to swallow the toothpaste or spit it into a towel.

Words for You

astronaut a member of the crew of a spacecraft

gravity the force that pulls objects toward one another

orbiting traveling in a circular path around an object in space

simulator a machine that imitates conditions for training purposes

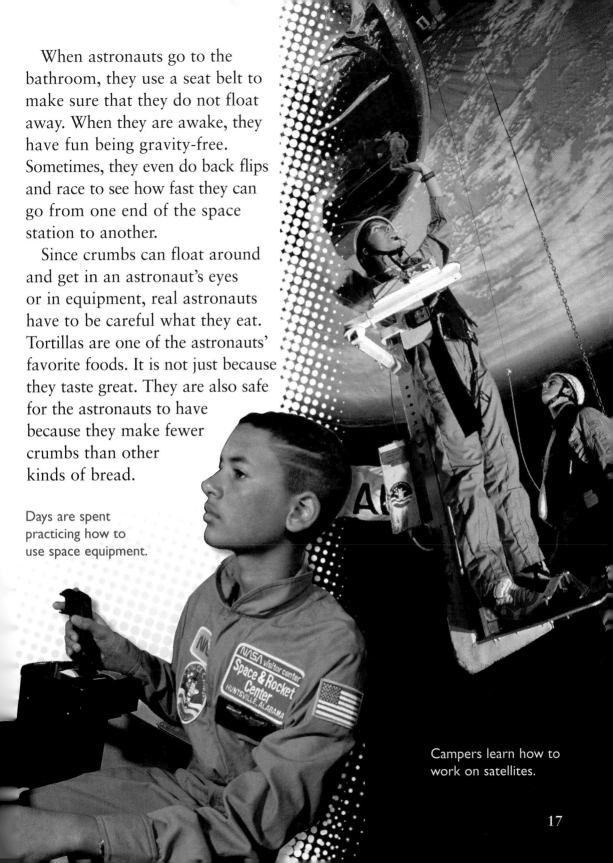

When astronauts go to the bathroom, they use a seat belt to make sure that they do not float away. When they are awake, they have fun being gravity-free. Sometimes, they even do back flips and race to see how fast they can go from one end of the space station to another.

Since crumbs can float around and get in an astronaut's eyes or in equipment, real astronauts have to be careful what they eat. Tortillas are one of the astronauts' favorite foods. It is not just because they taste great. They are also safe for the astronauts to have because they make fewer crumbs than other kinds of bread.

Days are spent practicing how to use space equipment.

Campers learn how to work on satellites.

17

Before leaving Space Camp, kids are sure to spend some time at Rocket Park. There, they can see the largest collection of rockets in the world. They'll also find a ride that takes them on a make-believe mission to Mars. Another ride shows what it feels like to take off in a space ship.

Visitors can watch movies that show what Earth looks like from outer space. Now, that's a real trip! So, if you want to become an astronaut one day—or just want to know what it feels like for five days during your summer break—then Space Camp may just be the right place for you.

Rocket Park

Down in Cajun Country

By Ben Kahn

Hands are clapping, and feet are stomping. A fiddler plays a fast tune. People greet each other with a language that sounds part French and part English. Spicy smells fill the air. Where are you? Why, you're down in Cajun Country!

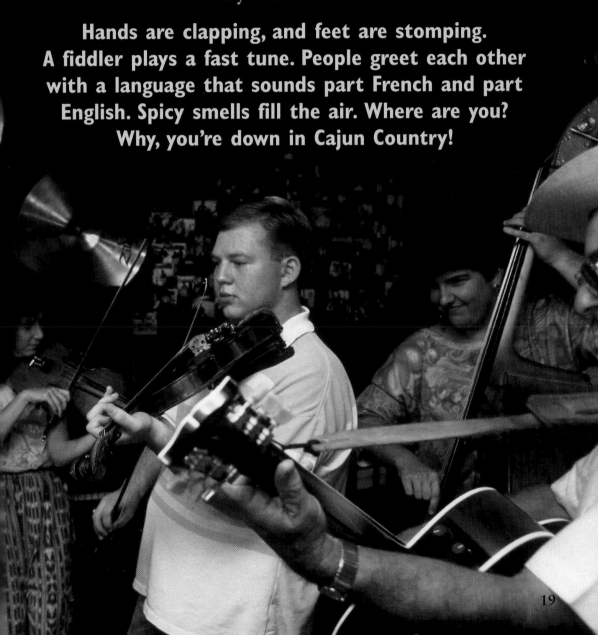

Who Are the Cajuns?

Today, Cajuns live in Louisiana near the coast and by the Mississippi River. Their ancestors came from France in the 1600s. They settled in a part of southeastern Canada called Acadia. Then, the British won a war with France and took over the area. The Acadians were forced to find new homes.

Many settled in southern Louisiana along the bayous, the streams that flow through the Mississippi River Delta region. The Delta has rich farmland that formed where the Mississippi River met the Gulf of Mexico. The Acadians farmed, fished for shrimp, and kept their old way of life. "Acadians" first got shortened to "Cadians" and later became "Cajuns."

Today, most Cajuns still live in the Mississippi Delta. They still farm and fish for shrimp, but many now work in the oil fields. Many Cajuns work on the oil rigs at sea. They often drill the first oil wells and train the workers. One thing that has not changed over time is their music. They play a special kind of music.

Catching crawfish

A traditional Cajun band

Cajun Music

Traditional Cajun music sounds sad and bluesy. Some people describe it as a nasal "holler." The main instrument used in Cajun music is the fiddle. Cajun fiddlers start playing when they are small children. Many famous fiddlers will tell stories about having carved a fiddle out of a wooden box that held crawfish.

The other instruments in a Cajun band are a steel guitar, push-button accordion, and steel triangle. The songs sung use French words. Many of the songs have been passed down in families. These songs were not written down. Singers memorized them.

In the late 1940s, Cajun music changed its sound. The musicians loved the rhythm and blues and jazz that they heard on the radio then. Bands stopped using the fiddle. Instead, they used a rubboard, a ridged steel vest worn over the chest. The musician uses thimbles or spoons to rub the board to make music. Some bands also add a saxophone. This music is called zydeco. Today, this kind of music is world-famous, with many festivals featuring zydeco music.

The Fais-Do-Do

One tradition that the Cajuns still practice today is called "fais-do-do" (FAY–doh–doh). The name means "go to sleep." Groups of families get together for trail-rides. Families ride horses, drive wagons, and invite costumed riders to join them. The families share food and music. They often will gather in parks along the river or in other public places. Then, they spend the long evening eating, dancing, playing cards, telling stories, and just having fun. While the grown-ups play, the babies sleep. That's why they call it a "fais-do-do."

Some of the food that they eat during a "fais-do-do" can include jambalaya. That is a spicy mix of rice, seafood, sausage, chicken, and vegetables. The one food you will definitely find there is crawfish. Crawfish are like little lobsters. You could say crawfish is the Cajun national dish!

Cajun French

Here are a few Cajun French words:

bayou (BI–oo) a slow-moving stream

fais-do-do a dance; literally means "go to sleep."

gumbo a soup or stew thickened with okra and seasoned with sassafras

jambalaya (jum–buh–LI–uh) a spicy dish of rice, seafood, sausage, chicken, and vegetables

lagniappe (LAHN–yop) a little something extra; an unexpected treat

pirogue (PEE–roh) a small, flat-bottomed Cajun canoe

zydeco (ZI–dih–koh) music that combines traditional Cajun music with rhythm and blues

Crawfish

Collecting Seashells

By Ricky Diaz

Do you like to collect things? Well, one thing that people in the Southeast collect is seashells. The shells are the homes of animals called mollusks. Mollusks are the second largest group in the animal kingdom. There are more than 150,000 different kinds of mollusks. That's a lot of shells to collect! And some of the most interesting shells are found in the Southeast.

23

The Southeast is famous for its many beaches. Different kinds of sea animals live in the waters along these beaches. Once they have shed their shells, the shells wash up on the beaches. People then collect the shells. You can find shells in the Southeast on rocky and sandy shores, in tide pools, and in marshes.

Shells have been used for many different purposes over the years in the Southeast. Native Americans used them for money and jewelry. Early settlers used the shells to pave roads and streets. Today, many gift shops in the Southeast sell seashells and different items, such as lamps, clothes, and magnets decorated with shells.

Tool Kit

Here is what you need for serious shell collecting:

tweezers to pry shells from rocks

stiff toothbrush to clean shells

magnifying glass to examine your finds

notebook and pen or pencil to write a description of each shell, and when and where you found it

plastic bag to store your shells

Seashells on the Seashore

Here are just a few of the shells you might find on the beaches of the Southeast.

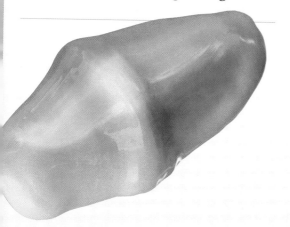

Lightning Whelk

These shells have jagged stripes that look a bit like lightning bolts.

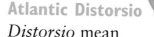

Atlantic Distorsio

Distorsio mean "distorted" or "twisted."

Tulip Shell

These shells can be found on coral reefs, seaweed, or sand.

Flamingo Tongue

This unusual shell is found on the southeast coast of Florida.

Pink Conch

Conch shells are popular in Florida. You may have seen them in movies.

Wandering Triton

Triton shells are named after the ancient Greek sea-god Triton.

The Legend of Casey Jones

By Becky Cheston

His real name was John Luther Jones, but he called himself Casey after Cayce, Kentucky, the town where he was born. Young Casey always knew just what he wanted—to be a railroad engineer.

Casey began as a brakeman—the fellow who brought the big locomotives to a full stop. Casey quickly worked his way up to fireman. Firemen kept the coal fires burning, producing the steam that powered the engine. In the summer of 1893, Casey finally got what he wanted. He was a locomotive *engineer*. Now, he drove the train.

Casey Jones in locomotive 638

In those days, a driver drove one train, and he stuck with his engine wherever it went. Casey's first locomotive was engine 638. Soon, people became familiar with Casey's signature whistle. He was also known for something else—lightning speed.

At that time, people never expected a train to be "on time." Railroad officials only asked that a driver make "running time." This meant, for example, that an engineer had to make a four-hour trip in four hours. He didn't have to make up any time that had been lost on previous runs. Casey didn't see things that way.

Casey pushed his crew—and his locomotive, now engine 382—to pick up speed down hills and along river bottoms. He often topped out at more than 80 miles an hour. Casey became known as a "highballer"—a risk-taking, high-speed driver. He may have been a locomotive hero to the train-riding public, but some other engineers had a different opinion.

"That Jones boy is showing off again," said an engineer one day as Casey sped past him. "And they don't pay a dime more for a fast run than they do for a good one."

27

Casey's Last Run

On April 30, 1900, Casey took over for another engineer on the run from Memphis, Tennessee, to Canton, Mississippi. It was a tricky run, with long, steep descents, and curves that seemed to come out of nowhere. Casey left Memphis about and hour and a half late. He was determined to make up the time.

Some historians say that he reached speeds of 100 miles an hour on this ill-fated run. The real problem began with two freight trains—engines 72 and 83—that were traveling in the opposite direction on the same track. When the two trains pulled off to a siderail, engine 83 stalled. It left four cars still sitting on the main track.

When Casey saw engine 83, his train was traveling at about 50 miles an hour. Both Casey and Sim Webb, his loyal fireman, knew they could not avoid a crash. Casey threw himself on the brakes, and yelled, "Jump, Sim, and save yourself!" He rode his engine into the stalled freight cars. Casey managed to cut his speed enough to save all his passengers and crew, but he was killed. Casey was found in the wreckage with one hand on the brake lever, the other on the whistle cord.

Casey Jones Today

At the time of his death, Casey Jones was living with his wife and children in Jackson, Tennessee. If you visit the Casey Jones Home and Railroad Museum there, you can walk through his house. Visitors can also climb aboard a model of engine 382.

Before you go, stroll over to the local cemetery and look at Casey's grave. His tombstone reads, "To the memory of the locomotive engineer whose name as 'Casey Jones' became a part of folklore and the American language."

Actual-size model of Casey Jones's locomotive

BUILDING THE FUTURE

By Gare Thompson

What do you do after you've been President of the United States? Former President Jimmy Carter helps to build homes. He and his wife Rosalyn live in Plains, Georgia, and each year they volunteer with Habitat for Humanity to build homes for the poor. In the summer of 2003, they built homes in Georgia and Alabama. For the Carters and others who live in small towns in the Southeast, it is a way to give back to their region.

Young volunteers for Habitat for Humanity

What Is Habitat for Humanity?

Habitat for Humanity is a worldwide nonprofit group that builds homes for the poor. Volunteers work together to build houses. The families that will live in these houses also must help to build their future homes.

The organization has built some 60,000 houses throughout the world. These homes have given shelter to about 300,000 people!

Jimmy Carter does more than drive nails. He also works to make people more aware of the need for houses that all people can afford.

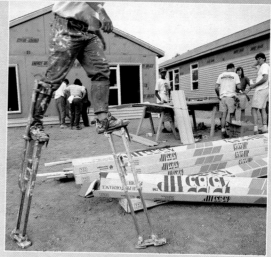
A team of volunteers

Many young people volunteer to work for Habitat for Humanity. Kids ages seven to ten help by planting trees and gardens. They help build too. Most importantly, they help introduce the children who move into the new home to the neighborhood.

Older kids ages ten to twelve often help by creating window boxes for the homes. The brightly colored boxes filled with flowers make a wonderful welcome for the new owners. Kids also help clean up the work site too. Throughout the Southeast, Habitat for Humanity and Jimmy Carter have been building the future. The homes they have built help people live better lives.

Former President Jimmy Carter

Insider's
Guide

Here are a few more special places that make the Southeast interesting and fun.

If you like getting wet, head to the **Chattahoochee River Recreation Area** just north of Atlanta, Georgia. It's one of the most popular places in the Southeast to canoe or simply float on a raft.

The Sea Islands off the Southeast's Atlantic Coast are the home of the African-American Gullah people. Each year, Beaufort, South Carolina, hosts a Gullah festival. It celebrates West African traditions of music, dancing, and storytelling.

Horse farms have been a part of Kentucky since it first became a state. **The Kentucky Horse Park** in Lexington, Kentucky, is a 1,200-acre park where you can see what all the horse excitement is about in Kentucky. The International Museum of the Horse is located here. You can also visit the Hall of Champions, which is where race-winning horses are shown to visitors.